How *not* to be a

Desperate Housewife

How to be a
not

Desperate Housewife

Charlotte Williamson

Illustrations by Veronica Palmieri

ROBSON BOOKS

First published in Great Britain in 2005 by Robson Books, The Chrysalis Building, Bramley Road, London W10 6SP

An imprint of **Chrysalis** Books Group plc

Text copyright © 2005 Charlotte Williamson
Illustrations copyright © 2005 Veronica Palmieri

British Library Cataloguing in Publication Data
A catalogue record for this title is available from the British Library.

ISBN 1 84340 336 6

Commissioning Editor: Victoria Alers-Hankey
Designer: Lotte Oldfield
Layout: e-digital

Reproduction by Classicscan, Singapore
Printed by CT Printing, China

Contents

Introduction

Picture the perfect housewife. The husband with the fat salary and super-stable job. The 2.4 children. The white picket fence. The matching headscarf and apron as she dusts the living room. The soufflés that always rise. The roast potatoes that effortlessly crisp on the outside yet remain soft on the inside. Is the perfect housewife happy? Is she heck.

If even the most uber of housewives have the odd wibble, then imagine how bad it is for the rest of us. Of course, the idea of being a Desperate Housewife is nothing new. Fifties housefraus fretted about keeping up with the Joneses while our mothers worried about all the baby goo-goo talk and mundane chores that might turn their educated minds to molten.

What is new, though, is the form this inner screaming takes. Modern housewife desperation is feeling unfulfilled. Inadequate. Paranoid. Brimming with envy. Dealing with working women who truly believe you've taken the easy option in life, staying at home keeping house. And it's a desperation that can strike even the sanest of people …

- Do you feel jealous of your nanny's youthful looks – and the way she so capably handles your children?

- Have you ever felt your household skills – cooking, cleaning, organising your family's routine – are woefully under par?

- Are you recently divorced and fear you will never meet a decent man again? Actually, make that *any* man again?

- You'll be serving a gourmet supper tonight only for it to be followed by another frosty reception from your husband in the bedroom?

- Would you ever be tempted to stray with the gardener?

If the above rings any bells, then lady, you're desperate. And you need help. Which is basically the idea behind this book.

We've divided the time-honored breed of housewife into four distinct types: the too-good-to-be-true Alpha Housewife, the frustrated from-boardroom-to-boredom BoBo Housewife; the arty yet ditzy Hippie Housewife and the money-minded Trophy Housewife.

We detail her household, her interior choices, what she has round her kitchen sink and what fills her bathroom cabinet. We delve into her love life, her family life, even her sex life before offering invaluable insider advice on how she can vastly improve her day-to-day existence. And stop being so desperate. The secret to a stress-free dinner party? Some new hot moves in the bedroom? It's soooo easy when you know how …

The Alpha Housewife

1

A throwback to the über-homemakers of
the fifties, the Alpha is the consummate
domestic goddess with the perfect
hair, perfect complexion, perfect Victoria
sponges … but a terrible marriage. Not
that her neighbours would know: for the
Alpha, it's all about keeping up appearances.

The Alpha: A Stepford Wife Extraordinaire

The Alpha is a Stepford Wife out of step with the modern world. She bakes her own cakes. She eats only in season, knowing the precise provenance of everything her family consumes. She makes her own wrapping paper *and* her own domestic cleaning products, and would happily have plastic dust covers on the soft furnishings if it weren't so un-chic. She thinks housework is hip – there's never a stray spider's web in her home – and has been known to run her finger idly over other people's mantelpieces. Dust is her number one nemesis.

Yes inside, the Alpha is crumbling. She is a total perfectionist, her quest for cleanliness an obsessive-compulsive disorder. Why else would she not allow the men of the house to pee standing up? Her marriage is falling apart and her kids resent her Victorian attitude to discipline. Still, there are so many photographs of her 'perfect family' scattered throughout her home that the neighbours would never know.

The Alpha has a ruthlessly competitive streak, that much is apparent – but really, who is she competing with other than herself?

Her cocktail

A Roaring Twenties-influenced Silk Stocking: made with tequila, crème de cacao and cream. Even the Alpha's tipple must be timeless.

Her knickers

Retro-referencing Agent Provocateur pink-and-black silk-satin panties with matching bra and suspender belt. After all that time, though, will Mr Alpha even notice.

Her shoes

Christian Louboutin stilettos: the spike heel and signature scarlet sole satisfy her dominatrix side, and are the perfect juxtaposition to her twinset-and-pearls.

Her handbag

A crocodile leather Kate Spade tote with Italian pig-suede lining. The Alpha simply adores Kate's upperclass New England aesthetic.

The Alpha Kitchen

The Alpha owns a pasta maker, ice-cream maker and ravioli cutter – and uses them all on a regular basis. Her cooker is a four-oven Aga, her fridge a limited-edition Smeg. Her daily loaf comes courtesy of a bread machine using recipes from the classic *Tassajara Bread Book*.

Welcome to the Alpha kitchen … and it's *purely* a kitchen: the Alpha is the only person in her neighbourhood to have both a separate pantry and laundry room. Labels are as important to her in this room as they are to other women in their wardrobe. Her units are genuine 1950s high-spec English Rose formica, red and white for the necessary overtones of an American diner. Her appliances are just as retro-looking: think a Kitchen Aid blender, Dualit toaster and Metrokane ice-o-mat Deco crusher, an exact replica of the 1939 original. And coasters, coasters everywhere – you can never have too many coasters. Well, the Alpha can't.

With her Mulberry leather Robert's radio tuned to a classical music station, she keeps this room totally spotless: she cleans around the corners of her windows with Q-tips, and makes her stainless steel sink shine by rubbing it with soda water before rinsing. Thank goodness, then, that there's a jar of Atrixo hand cream on the sill – it's not the most fancy of brands, she readily admits, but it's certainly the most effective.

How not to be Desperate Tip

The Alpha can cut down on her costly Diptyque habit by cooking brown sugar and cinnamon on a low heat. The house will instantly smell as if she's been baking all day.

The Alpha Bedroom

This room is so feminine and frou-frou that it's clear Mr Alpha hasn't had a lookin. The walls, for instance, are covered in exquisite Florence Broadhurst flock wallpaper – the Alpha's may have heard murals are all the rage now, but she could never let a muralist loose; she's a control freak, after all.

Boudoir style

The Alpha has covered her antique French sleigh bed (on which she continually stubs her toes, a typical sleigh-bed hazard) with the finest Irish linen which has a royal warrant, no less. Her nocturnal attire is just as elegant: a floor-skimming white cotton nightgown. A peach silk marabou-trimmed housecoat rests on her shoulders when she's reading in bed … alas, the most action this room sees these days.

How to do hospital corners

A duvet? How common! The Alpha is strictly sheets, for which she must master hospital corners – a neat freak's idea of heaven. Hospital corners are an exact science: first place the sheet squarely on the mattress. Tuck the foot and head ends tightly under the mattress. Then tuck in the two sides, all the while holding the corners out of the way. Pull tight and fold away the four corners. Perfection! If she were in the US Army, the Alpha would now be proudly bouncing a dime off the top.

What's on her nightstand?

Next to her hand-blown water decanter with matching glass is a neat stack of cookery books: for her, they're bedtime porn. At the moment she's especially fond of *The New English Kitchen* by Rose Prince, the foodies' cookbook du jour, anything by Martha Stewart or Mrs Beeton (her idols!) and *Extreme Cuisine* by Jerry Hopkins that includes recipes for iguana soup and '39 ways with crocodile'. Well, you never know.

Since Alpha's also an active member of the local book club, she's also ploughing through all the Oprah classics: think *One Hundred Years of Solitude* by Gabriel Garcia Marquez and *Heart of a Woman* by Maya Angelou. The Alpha also keeps a leather diary here to record her private thoughts – it naturally has a lock.

How not to be Desperate Tip

The Alpha likes to be alert from the moment she wakes up. A simple stretching exercise from the comfort of her bed should help: she needs to lie flat on her back and stretch her body in every direction, wiggling her hands and toes. She should also breathe deeply three or four times. Only now is she ready to face the world.

The Alpha Wardrobe

'Fashion fades, only style remains the same.' The Alpha lives by this Coco Chanel aphorism. She has a signature style – mid-century modern homemaker chic – adores brooches and has a penchant for pearls. *Much* more subtle than diamonds, she finds.

Her can't-live-without labels

- Diane Von Furstenberg. She loves the way the wrap dresses make her look neat in a jiffy. They're just as quick to remove – if Mr Alpha ever cared to try.

- Issa. A relatively new Brazilian designer whose floral silk-jersey dresses are just as easy to wear as DVF's, only with less recognizable prints.

- Hermes. A nattily tied scarf perfectly complements her style. The best are from Hermes; like the staff in the Paris flagship store, the Alpha knows at least 20 ways to tie one.

- Ballantyne. Traditional designs with a twist from the finest Scottish cashmere.

How not to be Desperate Tip

Try as she might, the Alpha can't control everything. Like her, moths have expensive tastes – and they *love* cashmere. If she spots one, she should place the affected garment inside a sealed plastic bag and put it in the freezer for three days to kill off lava. Of course, prevention is better than cure: moths loathe lavender, so she could put sachets in her wardrobe.

How to wash a cashmere twinset

Cashmere must be hand-washed. First, dissolve gentle soap flakes into lukewarm water. Soak the cashmere for 20 minutes. Rinse with lukewarm water until the water runs clear. Gently press out any excess moisture and then place the cashmere on a towel. Roll the towel up to remove any further water, then put the cashmere on a fresh towel, reshape and air-dry flat.

The Alpha Bathroom

The Alpha doesn't do anything as démodé as store her lotions and potions in the bathroom; instead, she uses a kidney-shaped dressing table from Clignancourt market in Paris, restored, repainted white and placed in her bedroom. Her makeup and Mason Pearson real-bristle brush lie next to a silver-framed photograph of her wedding day and a tuberose Diptyque candle. Her aesthetic aim? Nothing short of perfection.

The essentials ...

Lipstick: Pillow Talk from François Nars, a pretty azalea pink.
Moisturizer: D R Harris' Moisture Cream. In fact, she has several attractive bottles from D R Harris, an old-fashioned pharmacy in London, on display. **Scent:** Penhaligon's Bluebell – she loves the the royal warrant and the vintage packaging. **Her secret beauty tip:** Bliss Glamour Gloves, filled with a special moisturizing gel that works wonders on her hands while she's sleeping.

The honesty mirror

Since the Alpha prides herself on super-groomed perfection, she needs the most honest lighting possible for plucking brows and scrutinizing pores. In her dressing room, then – of course she has one! – is an 'honesty mirror' that perfectly illuminates her face. It needs to be lit from the sides, never from behind or the top, which can be done either with Hollywood-style bulbs or two 60-watt lamps, one on either side. Oh, and the best tweezers in the whole wide world? Slant-edged Tweezermans.

Squeaky-clean surfaces

The Alpha would never be happy here unless everything was hygienically just-so. For a clogged showerhead, she soaks the offending item in vinegar and then uses a large needle to declog the holes. For marks on the shower curtain, she machine-washes it with vinegar and a couple of towels to rub off the dirt, then dries it in the sun. And for the loo? Thankfully, that's never much of a problem – after all, the Alpha household mantra is: flush, brush, flush.

How not to be Desperate Tip

After all that housework, the Alpha should never neglect her hands. Exfoliating the backs with moist sea salt will instantly make them look better, as will applying hand cream at least twice a day. She should always wear rubber gloves for cleaning and cotton gloves for dusting. Applying a high-factor sunscreen is essential in sunny weather – alas, no surgery can stop this obvious sign of ageing. Who wants claws anyway?

The Alpha's Exercise Routine

Ever wondered how 1950s housewives stayed so slim? It was thanks to a heady mix of housework coupled with Dexedrine (essentially, legalized speed). The Alpha knows this, so she cranks up the stereo and transforms her chores into a series of exercises. Or should that be 'housercise'?

Improve muscle tone with a cloth

This move is great for improving lower-body strength. Keeping your upper body straight, hold your cloth with both hands firmly on the floor. Lunge forward on one leg while keeping the other leg straight or bending it towards the ground. Keep your arms straight ahead the whole time. Return to your original position, then repeat on the other leg.

Get strong with a sponge

This move improves upper-body strength. Lean over the side of the bathtub and polish ten times in one direction, applying as much pressure as possible. Repeat in the opposite direction.

The Alpha's Love and Sex Life

Love life? What love life? For the Alpha there's *married* life, sure, but there isn't much love. At least it seems that way most of the time. She needs to realize, though, that all is not lost: it's never too late to rescue a relationship …

Matrimonial SOS

Most psychologists agree that only 20 per cent of divorces are caused by an affair; the vast majority are due to marriages that simply fade away without a fight. While there are a million different ways in which a marriage can be happy, unhappy ones tend to have similar problems.

If the Alpha wants to salvage her marriage, she needs to start with herself. She must acknowledge there's a problem by reconnecting with her feelings of self-worth and realizing she deserves more. She should define the specific problems in her marriage, writing a list if that helps. She should realize, though, that no relationship is without problems. Absolutely none.

She should then speak to Mr Alpha. He, too, must admit there's a problem before they can both progress. If the Alpha recoils at the idea of talking face-to-face about their problems – such a controlling woman is probably going to loathe appearing vulnerable – she should write to her husband explaining in detail her feelings, making sure there is no room whatsoever for misinterpretation. She should remember what it was she loved about him in the first place, and suggest he does the same.

Finally, the Alpha would do well to remember that there are no rules about what does and does not constitute a good relationship. It's more about what works for the individual couple and makes them happy.

An Alpha sex life? Hardly ...

Sex could be what's wrong with the marriage. The Alpha is uptight around the house, so does that translate to the bedroom? Sort of – but Mr Alpha is far from keen on partaking in any conjugal relations these days, and when he does, she gets the distinct impression he would prefer things to be kinkier. Besides, she suspects he might be having an affair – could she be right?

It's easy for couples who've been married a long time to get complacent and lose interest in sex; indeed, the Alpha has probably convinced herself that a sexless marriage works for her. Deep down, though, she knows it doesn't – so this is yet another problem she needs to confront.

The C word

It's all about the C word: single girls crave commitment, while married ones are desperate for communication. Sometimes, even in the longest of marriages, couples can be embarrassed to say what they want sexually; what, in other words, turns them on.

One way round this thorny issue is the Communication Game. The Alpha should prepare a series of questions, some seemingly innocuous, others more probing, on separate pieces of paper, and put them in a hat. She should then invite Mr Alpha to play: pick a piece of paper and talk through his answer. All done, of course, when they're both relaxed. Below are some suggestions for the questions ... a few glasses of wine should help.

What are your highlights of our marriage so far?

What would you like to do more of?

What do you like most about me?

What did you like most about me when we first met?

What is your favourite sexual fantasy?

What most turns you on that I do?

Dealing with the other woman

Or rather, dealing with the affair, the cause of 20 per cent of divorces. The Alpha isn't actually sure her man is cheating. Short of hiring a private detective, though, she has two options: ignore the problem, in which case it can never be resolved, or confront him.

If her suspicions are correct, she should firstly remember that it's not her fault. Men have affairs for a variety of reasons, not just because their relationship is failing: it could be quick-fix sex; to boost his self-esteem; or simply because he was offered the chance. On the other hand, it could very well be because he's too cowardly to end his marriage and wants the Alpha to do it for him. She therefore needs to ascertain the exact reason *before* she can begin the healing process.

If Mr Alpha has made a mistake, she needs to tell him what he must do to win back her trust. The two of them should start spending more quality time together alone and remember: it's often said that affairs can make a couple stronger. If they both accept shared responsibility for eachother's happiness, the marriage could be even better than before

The Alpha needs to make the choice to forgive him – no one else can do this for her – but it doesn't mean she has to forget. However, if she *does* decide to forgive, she should try her best not to bring up the affair in any subsequent arguments. Not only is this proof that she *hasn't* forgiven him, but keeping scores is a sure-fire way to ruin any relationship.

The Alpha's Home Life

For the Alpha, everything in her home – the décor, the objects, even the people – must be the ultimate, the price one must pay for being an über-picky perfectionist. But, is achieving the ultimate ever really possible?

The ultimate temperament

Let's start with the Alpha herself. Her neighbours may act pleasantly towards her, they may respect her even, but do they actually like her? Might they be just a teeny bit scared?

Much of this intimidation is down to the Alpha's cut-throat attitude: she needs to be the best, needs to look down on others. If she wants to instantly improve her popularity, then, she must curb her competitiveness.

Women are generally most competitive towards other women, and indeed mums and housewives can be the worst: should you breastfeed? Go back to work after having a baby? Hire a nanny? The Alpha might have boasted about giving birth naturally – and it not hurting one bit. The same with breastfeeding: she might declare she was born to do it. She could also have bragged about her amazing diet about being the skinniest in her set. And don't get her started on her perfect family ...

Other cannier wives recognize this as a sign of deep-rooted insecurity, but does she? Constant competing can quickly get in the way of friendship. She needs to consider this to be a better – and less judgemental – girlfriend.

The ultimate packed lunch

On a happier note, the Alpha's perfectionism does have its occasional plus points. Her children may dislike her disciplinarian demeanour and limitations on TV viewing, but she does provide a delicious and nutritious packed lunch. It's her way of showing she cares. Here's one of her fabulous recipes as proof, which should be enough for two hungry children:

700g/1½lb brown rice, cooked
  and left to cool
75g/2½oz mozzarella
½ yellow pepper
½ tomato, seeded
4 radishes
2 spring onions
2 tbsp toasted pinenuts
50g/2oz mixed dried fruit:
  apricots, raisins, figs, etc.

For the dressing
Juice of 1 lime
2 tbsp extra virgin olive oil
2 tbsp finely chopped fresh
  flat-leaf parsley
2 tbsp finely chopped fresh mint
Salt and pepper to taste

Chop all the main ingredients into bite-sized pieces and mix well together. In a separate bowl, mix the dressing ingredients. Place both in separate sealed plastic containers. Mix the dressing with the salad before eating.

The ultimate teenagers

Oh, how she wishes she had some control over these! She doesn't understand the mood swings, the door slammings, anything – she was so well behaved when *she* was a girl, wasn't she?

Probably not. No teenager is an angel, partly because of madly fluctuating hormones, partly because new research has proven moody, erratic behaviour has much to do with their brains – not only is the human brain still growing during adolescence (and possibly even more than it does during early childhood) but is also undergoing some radical rewiring, particularly in the part that governs logic and controls emotions. Short of a lobotomy, then, there's not much she can do. Other than relax.

The ultimate household pet

Although the Alpha thinks pets in general are filthy beasts, she'll make a special concession for a Savannah. The Savannah is the current 'It' pet (last year's was the Bengal – *do* keep up), a cross between a wildcat – the African Serval – and a domestic cat. The result is the largest domestic breed to date – so large, in fact, that it can be taken for walks on leads. It has already been banned from many US states.

Due to its exclusivity, the Alpha would thoroughly indulge her Savannah: feed it freshly cooked fish; take it to special feline spas for pampering; even consider cloning it. Really, though, the Alpha's ultimate pet should be a Labrador. Why? Because a loyal dog would offer her unconditional affection, something she doesn't receive from her family.

The ultimate ultimate: How to be happy

Surely, this is everyone's ultimate aim in life, yet the Alpha is further from achieving this than most. She could start by trying to be less of a control freak. It's a little odd how she finds housework relaxing and meditative as opposed to merely a chore. She thinks nothing of cleaning the fridge at midnight or scrubbing the bathroom at 2am. If her husband finds her, she'll feel naughty, as if she's been doing something illicit. Seriously, what is she hiding?

Being a germaphobe is the Alpha way of finding order in our chaotic world. She needs to take the advice of Joan Rivers, who once said: 'I hate housework! You make the beds, you do the dishes – and six months later, you have to start all over again!'

Alpha Entertaining

She's the only wife on the block who doesn't dread the phrase 'A dinner party for six'. To really impress this time, the Alpha has plumped for a picnic. In reality, though, it's more of an alfresco feast, presented in a bulging wicker basket and served using the finest bone china. Always the consummate hostess, she's even remembered posies for each place 'sitting' on the rug. Her guests are understandably impressed.

What to do

She knows all about the importance of picnic one-up(wo)manship. Everything she serves is in season and sourced locally – and boy, does she make sure all her guests know.

The Alpha has decided to serve sandwiches, macaroons, a basket of fresh berries and iced tea kept cool in a thermos. She knows everything tastes better in the fresh air but it still has to be perfect. The sandwiches should be dainty with bread that's been cut very thin and the crusts removed. The cucumber sandwiches should contain thinly sliced cucumber that has been peeled and sprinkled with white wine vinegar 20 minutes before being made. Ham is best shredded; garnish with mustard and a lettuce leaf. Egg should be mashed with butter after being hard-boiled. Add salt, pepper, a squeeze of lemon and some finely chopped spring onions.

How not to be Desperate Tip

Relax, as this will make her guests relax. If she's uptight, they're uptight.

Alpha Menu

Simply marvellous almond and vanilla macaroons

Makes about 30
115g/4oz sifted icing sugar
75g/2½oz finely ground almonds
Seeds from 1 vanilla pod
White of 1 large egg

For the filling
75g/2½oz mascarpone
75g/2½oz greek yoghurt
1 tbsp sifted icing sugar

Mix the sugar, almonds and vanilla in a bowl. In another bowl, whisk the egg white until it reaches a stiff peak, then fold it into the almond mixture using a metal spoon. Scoop into a piping bag and pipe 3cm diameter rounds on to a baking tray lined with parchment. Flatten slightly. Leave to stand until a film forms – this could take up to 30 minutes – and then bake in an oven at 100ºC/225ºF/Gas 4 for 45 minutes. Leave to rest for five minutes before transferring to a wire rack. Mix together the filling ingredients and use to sandwich two macaroons together.

An elegant iced tea

Put the tea leaves in the water and leave overnight. In the morning, strain the liquid into a vacuum flask. Add a slice of lemon and a couple of ice cubes before serving.

25g/1oz tea leaves
1 pint cold water
1 lemon, sliced
Ice cubes

Alpha Escapes

Since she already spends her spare time making macramé wall hangings and restoring picture frames, it's hardly surprising that the Alpha prefers a holiday during which she can learn a new skill. And sporting holidays? Well, these simply launch the Alpha's competitive spirit into a whole new sphere.

1. Cooking

Where? At the Raymond Blanc Cookery School at Le Manoir aux Quat Saisons.

Why? Amateur chefs rave about this cookery school and meals at the adjoining Michelin-starred restaurant should inspire her.

The programme: Lessons are from 9am until 4.30pm, when students relax over afternoon tea to discuss their progress. During the four-day course, most aspects of food preparation are covered.

What should she wear? Think Nigella Lawson – after all, the Alpha already prides herself on their similar wardrobes – with a lilac cashmere twinset, long skirt and free-flowing hair.

What will give her the edge? Bringing her own Divertimenti spatula.

2. Tennis

Where? The Algarve at the Jonathan Markson Tennis Camp.

Why? On the Portuguese coast, the Algarve offers plenty of sunshine to prompt even the laziest of players on to the courts.

The programme: The course promises to develop a player's 'killer instinct'. One stroke is concentrated on per day; it's intensive so there's no time for sunbathing.

What should she wear? Whites – she likes pretending she's at

Wimbledon – and New Balance trainers, the chicest sneakers around. **What will give her the edge?** A Wilson racquet: the tennis snob's favourite.

3. Watercolour painting

Where? In the Tuscan Hills with Battina Schroeder Painting Holidays.

Why? Schroeder, who has been organizing painting trips since the early 1980s, chooses Europe's prettiest vistas for her students – only the best for the Alpha.

The programme: Lessons daily to improve on brushwork, composition and colour, accompanied by a delicious picnic.

What should she wear? A full-length, buttoned-through linen dress, floppy straw hat and fey smile.

What will give her the edge? A complete set of red sable brushes.

The Alpha Garden

The Alpha always attends to her garden. Martha Stewart-style, with trug in hand and hair tied back in a scarf. She has the poshest plants on the block and has done her darnedest to replicate an entire country meadow in a few square metres. Somewhat surprisingly, she's *almost* pulled it off. If only her neighbours would care as much about their street's appearance.

Her horticultural aim

She wants an old-fashioned cottage garden that becomes a riot of colour in the summer. (Naturally, she has visited Chawton Cottage, Jane Austen's house with the quintissential English country garden, where she took notes and made numerous sketches.) Her house may have been built in the 1980s but her garden is pure 18th century – and she doesn't understand why connoisseurs would consider this just a teeny bit jarring.

Perfect plants

A cottage garden should look artless; of course, it's not. All those crowded-together flowers require considerable care: constant cutting back and deadheading. Still, the Alpha loves a challenge. Traditional cottage garden blooms include poppies, lupins, delphinium, larkspur and tumbling roses as well as smaller plants like cornflowers, nasturtium, convolvulus and scabious, planted in a carefully considered collection of reclaimed Victorian sinks and planters. The Alpha also loves foxgloves but they don't love her – she's been getting complaints from her neighbours because they've been spreading over the boundaries. The Alpha can't control everything, it would seem.

The Alpha Mission Statement

I .... knowingly identify myself as
an **Alpha Housewife**. And I am **DESPERATE**.

•••••••••••

I hereby acknowledge my faults: that I am uptight,
uber-conservative, fiercely competitive, and something of
a cold fish.

•••••••••••

I do solemnly declare that in order to be less desperate, I
will curb my perfectionism. That alone will drastically
improve my life. •

•••••••••••

In five years time I will have learnt how to chill out,
maybe even taking a leaf out of the Hippie's book and
starting yoga. That way I'll appreciate my family and
friends so much more – and they'll appreciate me.

•••••••••••

•••••••••••

And if I achieve my goals, I will treat myself (and only me) to … an epicurean tour of Italy, starting in the north with the white truffles of Piedmont, and travelling down through Bologna, Parma, and Tuscany – taking in the Faith Willinger cooking school that includes market-to-table sessions, all done in an eighteenth-century kitchen in the middle of Florence – ending up in Bra, the capital of the Slow Food Movement. Which, quite frankly, will be the first time in my Alpha life that I've ever slowed down.

•••••••••••

The BoBo Housewife

2

BoBo means 'From Boardroom to Boredom'. Here's a housewife who used to work in the City; these days, however, with four uncontrollable kids under five, the only reminder of her high-powered past is her corporate wardrobe now covered in baby drool. The BoBo's one saving grace is the still-healthy relationship she has with her husband. Well, just about …

The BoBo: From boardroom to boredom

'I used to have a job,' she sighs at a neighbourhood play-date, mindlessly tapping a tambourine to the strains of 'The Wheels on the Bus …' Meanwhile, her four boys – all under five – run riot. Thanks to her former high-flying salary, she still has smart clothes and sleek interiors, albeit somewhat child-scratched around the edges. She also has a healthy marriage, yet pangs of jealousy directed at her husband's still-thriving career are an occasional strain. In short, the BoBo has a sharp mind fast turning to jelly – which, incidentally, she now makes incessantly for a plethora of tea parties she now attends.

Children transform some career women into earth mothers, while other once-utterly-unambitious mums find themselves itching to start their own business. The BoBo is a breed between the two. Although her mother may have fought against the tyranny of domestic drudgery, the BoBo has taken the post-feminist stance of becoming a modern stay-at-home mum. Unfortunately, no one told her it would be so dull, or so hard.

She has photos stuck on her stainless-steel Maytag Trilogy fridge-freezer (which used to be concealed, minimalist-style, until she forgot which door it was behind) of her housewife heroines, Meryl Streep and Demi Moore: power actresses who gave up their careers for kids but, crucially, have since resumed them, something the BoBo finds reassuring. If only she could run her household as well as she ran her office, the BoBo wouldn't feel quite so frazzled.

Her cocktail

A Smoking Martini: four parts Grey Goose vodka, one part scotch, four drops of Pernod. The BoBo loves the name because it encompasses two former vices in one.

Her knickers

One hundred per cent cotton boy-leg briefs, usually by laid-back Aussie label Bonds – although she *has* been known to steal her sons' when resources run low …

Her shoes

Pony skin Marni clogs, her concession to femininity and a reminder of the late 1990s when she had money to burn. She often teams them with three-quarter-length chinos and a white shirt.

Her handbag

A classic roomy Bill Amberg affair, another reference to her bygone corporate days. Half a sandwich languishes at the bottom – she has no idea of its age or provenance.

The BoBo Kitchen

These days, the BoBo spends much of her time here. It never used to be the case. This once-sleek bespoke John Pawson-designed, Belgian-constructed kitchen from Obumex was utterly pristine because she only ever ate out.

Alas, now it's all multi-this and multi-that. The BoBo's kitchen is no longer cutting edge; instead, its surfaces are crowded with multi-tasking, multi-purpose gadgets. She has a Magimix Cuisine Systeme 5100, for instance, a mixer that does about ten different things at once, and a Tefal steamer that cooks an entire meal in one go. So dull. Practical used to be a word she loathed; these days, it's strictly substance over style.

How to run your household like a PLC

Since the BoBo used to run her office so well, surely she can apply the same rules of business to her household? As a mum, she's automatically project manager. Her aim is to maximize her profit: make her house run as smoothly as she can with minimum fuss.

She therefore needs to share the load and delegate chores to the kids, explaining clearly what she expects from each task and providing rewards – chocolate buttons, perhaps? Like any good manager, she should also praise in public but criticize – scold – in private.

If a corporate consultant were brought in, he'd recommend she become her own PA, setting aside a dedicated day each week to do the following: pay bills, plan chores, organize a schedule, remember 'me' time – maybe Sunday evenings? To save time, she could even keep a shopping list stuck to the fridge door and cross off items as she runs low.

If none of this works, though, she wonders: can she make an executive decision to cut her losses and leave?

The BoBo Bedroom

The BoBo's bedroom is a bit of a surprise. Since it's her sanctuary, she makes this area as calm, restful and devoid of clutter as possible. The result? Something akin to a hip hotel room painted periwinkle, the most soothing of boudoir shades. She *even* has a pair of uplighters by the bed.

Comfort zone

The BoBo does everything in her power to have a blissful night's sleep, so she's invested in the best mattress available on the market, pocket-sprung and with a completely natural filling. Speaking of natural, her duvet must be goose-down, preferably Hungarian or Siberian, which are lightest. Her pillows should also be natural and square-shaped, the most comfortable for both reading and a good night's sleep. As for the sheets, her former taste of the high-life means she's no stranger to the 1200 thread count (yes, it *can* go that high) Egyptian cotton sheet. The BoBo's canny enough not to get swayed by thread count one-upmanship – she knows that good sheets are thanks to a number of other factors such as the quality of the yarn. That's why she's so faithful to Frette, the company known for the best sheets in the world. And the bedspread? In keeping with the hotel theme, it simply has to be waffle and from The White Company.

A lavender marriage

As tempted as the BoBo is to reach for the pharmaceuticals, she's decided, for the sake of her frazzled sanity, to experiment with more holistic methods. When she wants some instant 'me time', she reaches for a hot-pink meditation cushion stuffed with

lavender from Holistic Silk. For an undisturbed night's sleep she slips a couple of heated mini-cushions – again filled with lavender – into her pillows, courtesy of traditional English herbalist Culpeper. Aaaaah.

What's on her nightstand?

Whatever's just won the Booker so she can stay in the dinner-party loop: she accepts that she will never, ever finish it but will know page one by heart. Also, a bottle of Molton Brown's Air of Sleep containing bergamot and yup, you guessed it, more lavender, which she spritzs with abandon.

How not to be Desperate Tip

The BoBo should stop wearing that faded Mickey Mouse T-shirt to bed – or her husband might stop fancying her. One old-school but oh-so-sexy option is a pair of men's silk PJs from Brioni. The result: *very* Kate Hepburn.

The BoBo Wardrobe

The BoBo may have swapped her sporty soft-top for an SUV but she's stuck with the same corporate clothes: preppy separates (now covered in baby sick) and sensible shoes. Her cocktail dresses are gathering cobwebs: when will she ever have the chance to wear them now?

Her can't-live-without labels

- LL Bean. Americans do preppy best and LL Bean, the company that actually invented the canvas tote, is her favourite. She especially loves their online customization service.

- J&M Davidson. For simple summer dresses and classic fitted jackets.

- Paul Smith. Structured, clean lines – it's what she relies on for the rare occasions she dresses up.

- Turnbull and Asser. The famous British shirtmakers do both ready-to-wear and bespoke women's wear, the Bobo's one remaining indulgence is a tailor-made shirt.

Storage solutions

Since the rest of the house is in perpetual chaos, she tries to keep her own mess as minimal as possible. Clothes, therefore, should be put away the moment they're discarded. She should fold jumpers, T-shirts, shirts and anything particularly fine or delicate – in an ideal world she would use tissue paper to minimize creasing, but seriously, does she have the time? Suits, dresses and trousers must all be hung, the latter using special hangers. In fact, Joan Crawford was right: 'No wire hangers ever!' She therefore sticks to wooden or, for very delicate fabrics, satin-padded. To achieve maximum storage-savvy merit points, the BoBo should finally separate her summer wardrobe from her winter, and vacuum-pack any out-of-season outfits.

The BoBo Bathroom

The BoBo is a proponent of the no-fuss, no-nonsense look, so she needs products that work well – and fast. She swears she hasn't painted her nails once in the past five years. No time, you see. Still, she makes the odd effort for Mr Bobo – not to say herself – by ensuring she's never *too* hirsute.

The essentials

Lipstick: Bahama Mama, a nearly nude shade from Benefit. **Moisturizer:** Dermalogica Skin Smoothing Cream. She's also a fan of their facials: their beauticians will run through a list of causes for all her post-teenage spots – on the jawline equals stress, for instance; the nose, pollution; the chin, diet; and so forth. **Scent:** Cefiro by Floris, a fruity unisex fragrance she can share with her husband. **Her secret beauty tip:** Eye Patch Therapy from Parisian eye-care specialists Talika which will instantly refresh her eyes and reduce dark circles.

Five thoroughly self-indulgent treats

Here's a housewife desperately in need of some girly treats …

1. Jessica Pedicures are positively orgasmic since they include a sensational foot massage using aromatherapy-based products.

2. The most relaxing facials *by far* are those without any extractions. Elemis Fruit Active Glow facial perks up dull skin and uses massage techniques instead of squeezing to remove any

impurities. With those exotic-smelling lotions and relaxing panpipe music, the BoBo could almost be in Bali.

3. The BoBo's bath is her one escape. She can quickly transform it into a mini flotation tank with Deep Relax Bath Oil by Aromatherapy Associates.

4. Tocca Crema da Corpo is the silkiest body lotion out there. Perfect for some post-bath pampering.

5. Ayurvedic massages use gorgeous-smelling oils but aren't that firm – it's more like being stroked, in fact. Thai massages, on the other hand, will yank her shoulders back into shape.

Homeopathic alternatives to Ritalin

The BoBo has been known to borrow the kids' drugs when she needs to calm down. Understandable, really, but far from ideal. Homeopathic alternatives are much bette: both valerian and passiflora are renowned for their sedative qualities and are readily available in capsules from most health food shops. She would also do well to implement a 'no caffeine after 2pm' rule that includes coffee, tea and chocolate.

How not to be Desperate Tip

The BoBo should keep a bottle of cleanser in the kitchen. That way she can remove the day's grime – *and* save time – while she is busy preparing the evening meal.

The BoBo's Exercise Routine

Boxercise, a form of exercise that uses boxing moves mixed with aerobics, puts the BoBo in touch with her more aggressive, masculine side – really, what better way is there to vent her frustrations than punching in time to music? It does wonders for her upper body strength, too – not that lugging family-sized drink containers from the supermarket hasn't helped too – and also gives her a chance to mingle with humans who actually drive cars, as opposed to play choo-choo with them.

The straight punch

1. Stand with your knees slightly bent, left foot forward (or right foot if you're left-handed) and body weight equally distributed.

2. Form both hands into fists, with your thumbs tucked around the outside of your fingers, not inside.

3. Move your right hand up towards your chin, as if protecting your face, while punching straight forward with your left hand.

4. Keep your left arm at shoulder height while punching and move your body weight on to your left foot.

5. Now move your left hand up to your chin and punch with your right fist, again moving your body weight forward on to your left foot as you do so. Keep alternating punches in this way.

The hook

1. Stand with your body weight equally distributed and your fists clenched in the same way as for straight punching.

2. Move your right hand up to just under your chin, as if protecting your face.

3. Turn your left fist over, palm facing down, and punch in a circular motion across the front of your body. Simultaneously, pivot your feet and hips in the direction of the punch. Imagine connecting with all four knuckles.

4. Keep your left elbow at the same level or slightly lower than your fist, and move your body weight on to your left foot as you punch.

5. Now move your left hand up to your chin and punch with your right fist, this time pivoting your body in the opposite direction. Keep alternating punches in this way.

The BoBo Love and Sex Life

The BoBo has by far the best marital relationship in her neighbourhood. By *far*. Still, she'd need regressive therapy if she were to recall anything resembling a honeymoon period. Sure, her and Mr BoBo are the best of friends, but they need to get back to that boyfriend/girlfriend phase. Something that calls for more dates. A quick-fix date solution could be the BoBo sending the children to bed early while her hubbie makes some space in his electronic organizer – even if it's just an hour together in the bath.

When those women's magazines start making sense

Much to the BoBo's horror, she's found herself in the doctor's waiting room avidly reading the problem pages of weekly women's magazines, in particular the tips on 'Keeping the relationship flame alive'. She has also been taking notes – a woman with an MBA, no less.

They suggest sending a husband a heartfelt card, leaving love notes in his packed lunches or suit pockets, or doing one of his mundane chores – such as mowing the lawn – as a surprise. They also advise that a wife should make more of an effort with her appearance, freshening up and putting on a little makeup before he returns home from the office. She knows it's achingly antiquated, as if feminism never happened, but deep down it makes sense. The BoBo readily admits she occasionally needs reminding that, although her kids come first, the relationship between her and her husband is the singularly most important one in the family.

Long-term lovin'

Sex is super-complicated when there are children around – privacy, tiredness, can't-really-be-botheredness – but it absolutely mustn't stop. All those lovely endorphin and seratonin chemicals swimming round her body will help the BoBo relax if nothing else. Some women's-magazine-style tips should help here too …

1. Perfect the art of the quickie. Have no time for intimate relations? Spontaneously grab him in the linen cupboard or round the back of the garden shed. How thrilling!

2. (Almost) indecent exposure. Sex in semi-public places is guaranteed to spice up your love life. Although any prospective private schools you've registered children for might frown upon parents with a criminal record …

3. Set your alarm early. Aim for 20 minutes earlier than usual for a dose of first-thing fumbling.

4. Make like Mr and Mrs Smith. Book a babysitter and then arrange to meet in a hotel. Separately.

5. Share fantasies. If they're on the right side of deviant, act them out too. When you think you really know someone, you naturally start taking them for granted. Hearing their innermost thoughts, however, will prove you don't. If you think about it, you never really know anyone completely – now, how sexy is that?

Nature's Aphrodisiacs

Too-tired-for-sex syndrome. Aaah, the BoBo knows that only too well. The combination of children, housework and Mr BoBo's job means that relations aren't quite as frequent as they could be. All is not at a loss, though, since certain foods can work wonders on even the weariest of libidos …

1. Oysters. Casanova was said to have eaten 50 raw oysters every morning – using a girl's breast as his plate, no less – to improve his sexual prowess. There's scientific proof, too, since the high zinc content helps regulate the testosterone levels (semen is actually full of zinc).

2. Chocolate. Casanova adored this as well – he religiously ate a generous chunk before every one of his numerous encounters. Chocolate contains the chemical theobromine, a proven aid to arousal, while another chemical, phenylethylamine, produces the same fuzzy feelings human's experience when they're in love.

3. Truffles. The musty scent of this fungus contains chemicals similar to the sex hormones found in the male pig – stay with us here – which is why farmers only send female pigs out to snuffle for truffles. Curiously, these hormones are also similar to the sex hormones found in men, hence their aphrodisiacal quality. Many women, on the other hand, actually find the scent a turn-off.

4. Vanilla. Another scent that sends men wild – scientific research proves this is the smell males find most seductive.

The BoBo's Home Life

If she's completely honest, the BoBo only really has three problems, but boy, what problems: feral children, nanny issues and regular pangs of jealousy when she thinks about Mr BoBo's career. Try as she might to be the happy hausfrau, she inevitably spends her days desperate. Still, she can deal with these issues if she thinks of her home life in the business terms she's familiar with – or rather, as a series of business mantras ...

'Fake it 'til you make it': The modern way to reprimand children

The BoBo's badly behaved children rule the roost. They're rowdy, demanding constant attention, and she blames herself entirely – unlike her mother, she's decided never to smack them. Lately, though, she's been thinking that spanking might be the only option that works. Luckily, it's not.

Reprimanding children is all about maintaining authority and gaining control. One method she could try is to adopt a persona and alternate her voice. When she's telling them off, for instance, she should aim for a low, measured tone and use eye contact – in other words, get down on their level. She should tell them that their behaviour is unacceptable and, more importantly, explain why. On the other hand, if her brats are being well behaved for once she should raise her voice and adopt a sunny, smiley tone. Easy, no?

Another concept that many modern mothers swear by is the 'naughty step', a specially designated punishing spot away from the main action. The BoBo should always give children one last chance before sending them there. The naughty step is the last resort.

The BoBo should also start a regimented routine – children crave this. She can even encourage them to help with her tasks – bringing in the washing, for example – as well as factoring in time for herself. Soon, she'll no longer be faking it; in fact, she'll be a bone fide supermum.

'The greater the artist, the greater the doubt': The dos and don'ts of hiring a nanny

Naturally, the BoBo has her doubts about hiring a nanny. She's a stay-at-home mum, so surely she should be able to cope on her own? More importantly, what if her husband gets the hots for the nanny?

These doubts are understandable. If she does decide to go ahead and hire a modern-day Mary Poppins, though, there are certain attributes the BoBo should look for: someone who likes children and enjoys playing with them, who is trustworthy and organized, and who will respect the rules and belief system of the house.

Likewise, the BoBo must show her nanny the necessary respect. She needs to be laid-back when it comes to her nanny's methods of childrearing – that's why she's hired her, after all – and be prepared to feel intruded upon.

Ah yes, the nightmare scenario of being unable to hide *anything* from the nanny, as countless tabloid exposés have proved. Nannies see everything and can feel any spousal tension. They will, of course, gossip, but hopefully only to other nannies they meet at the playground.

And her final doubt: her husband falling for the nanny – or vice versa. Classic clues include the nanny showing him endless attention and only ironing his shirts … all the while refusing to look the lady of the house in the eye. If it bothers the BoBo that much – and it could – then there's always the male nanny option.

'A bend in the road is not the end of the road': Dealing with feelings of jealousy over her husband's still-thriving career

Otherwise known as the BoBo's belief that she's completely lost her identity. Nowadays, she's just someone's mum or someone's wife, *not* an individual, which is why she occasionally finds herself uncontrollably jealous of her husband's life outside the home: the fact he has work clothes, work friends – heck, she's even envious of his commute.

The BoBo needs to get out more. One solution is to return to work part-time – not all women are cut out to be stay-at-home mothers, after all. Alternatively, she could start her own business from the relative comfort of her kitchen table. That's exactly what the women behind the fashion label Juicy Couture did when they recognized a gap in the market for maternity jeans. Now, they've branched out and their company is worth millions – something that would never have happened if they hadn't become mums. A fitting lesson for the BoBo.

BoBo Entertaining

The BoBo has a sophisticated palate. She is – well, *was* – used to fine dining after all, and has no qualms about cooking: she knows homemade food inevitably tastes best. But alas, she doesn't always have the time. The solution for dinner parties, then, is a one-pot dish, preferably a recipe that can be made in advance, even if it means staying up until 2am the night before to finish it.

What to do

The BoBo must first clear away all the children's clutter – a miniature train set is hardly conducive to good dinner party conversation, is it? The right flowers will instantly freshen a room, and freesias have a particularly seductive scent.

She should then think about how she can make the most of some precious adult company – at last hurrah! A few carefully chosen party games should help set her back into adult gear. For intance, the Name Game, which requires each guest to write down the names of five famous people on five pieces of paper and put the names into a hat. The BoBo then divides her guests into two teams. Each team has 30 seconds to come up with the name produced from the hat with only a team member's clues for help. The team with the most right answers wins.

Too much strain on the brain for one night? Well, there's always Twister.

BoBo Menu

One-pot chilli con carne

Heat the oil in a heavy-bottomed saucepan and cook the bacon until crisp. Remove the bacon and set aside. Add the garlic and then brown the mince over a medium heat for 5–7 minutes. Add the chilli, cumin, cinnamon and pepper and stir. Add the onion soup and bacon and cook for 5 minutes. Stir in the chopped tomatoes, tomato paste and purée and cook, uncovered, over a gentle heat until the liquid is reduced (about 35 minutes). Add the beans towards the end, making sure they are heated through. Serve rolled up in a hot tortilla with sour cream, guacamole and salad.

3 tbsp vegetable oil
4 rashers streaky bacon,
   cut into strips
2 cloves garlic, chopped
500g/1lb 2oz organic beef mince
2 tsp chilli powder
2 tsp ground cumin
Pinch of ground cinnamon
½ tsp ground black pepper
400g/14oz canned French onion
   soup – no need to chop onions!
400g/14oz canned chopped
   tomatoes
200g/7oz tomato paste
150g/5oz can tomato purée
400g/14oz can red kidney beans,
   drained

Drop-dead gorgeous guacamole

Peel and pit the avocados. Mash with a fork. Stir in the remaining ingredients. Eat!

3 ripe avocados
1 small onion, finely chopped
3 red peppers, deseeded and
   chopped finley
2 garlic cloves, crushed
Pinch of cumin powder
1 tsp lemon juice
Salt and pepper to taste

BoBo Escapes

The BoBo loves a hip boutique hotel or converted grand mansion, the less child-friendly, the better. Hurrah, then, for the occasional romantic get-away with her husband, which also offers her the chance to indulge in her twin passions for luxury sheets and gourmet cuisine.

1. Paris

Where? Hotel Costes.

Why? This hotel has a dangerously sexy atmosphere: lots of deep red furnishings and dark, dark lighting. Perfect in winter.

Fantasy role-play: Vanessa Paradis. Johnny Depp first caught sight of her – or rather, her back – in the Costes bar.

Amorous activities: Hide and seek behind the statues of the Musée Rodin, surely the most romantic museum in the world.

Where to eat: If courtyard dining at Costes seems too sceney, she'll want to find the ultimate Parisian bistro instead. Le Bon Saint Pourcain in the shadow of Saint Sulpice comes close.

And later? The rooms are dark as well (thanks to dimmers and candles) and decorated in a manner that befits the 18th-century exterior. Oooh, and the hotel baths are big enough for two.

2. Venice

Where? Hotel Gritti Palace overlooking the Grand Canal.

Why? A close rival to Paris in the city-of-lovers stakes, Venice has many grand hotels. The Gritti Palace has charm in spades, which makes it more romantic still.

Fantasy role-play: Julie Christie in *Don't Look Now*.

Amorous activities: A sunset gondola ride on the Grand Canal.

Where to eat: Harry's Bar, the legendary canal-side café that invented both the bellini and beef carpaccio. Also perfect for people-watching.

And later? The rooms are like stepping into a fairytale: dazzling chandeliers and gilt mirrors complement the chintzy antiques.

3. Fiji

Where? Wakaya, a private island resort in tropical Fiji, that contains just nine cottages. The ultimate island hideaway.

Why? This is where Bill Gates spent his honeymoon, and if it's good enough for one of the richest men in the world …

Fantasy role-play: Nellie Forbush in *South Pacific* singing 'Some Enchanted Evening' as the sun goes down.

Amorous activities: A couples' pampering session at the spa following a hard day on the hammock.

Where to eat: The organic restaurant includes visiting chefs – Nobu Matsuhisa (aka Mr Nobu) has been one, something that should give an indication of the gourmet quality. Better still, take a picnic basket and two-way radio and dine in solitude under the stars.

And later? After an outdoor shower à deux, the BoBo can look forward to slipping between some fancy Italian sheets.

The BoBo Garden

Slides, swings, a makeshift football pitch: the BoBo's garden is hardly a haven. In truth, she never had any interest in gardening until she became a housewife. Now she's hooked and scans easy-grow guides when she gets the odd moment to herself. She prefers plants she can eat: for a beginner, an obvious end result can be more satisfying.

Her horticultural aim

Even though she now lives in the heart of suburbia, the BoBo still hankers for a practical urban-style garden that, alas must be child-friendly too. However, she's cleverly sectioned off a small 'no trespassing' space where she can experiment with herbs and vegetables. Luckily, her children refuse to eat their greens, so, for once, they're not even tempted to meddle

Perfect plants

A tough strain of grass for the lawn – in other words, one that can withstand rowdy ball games. That's the boring bit. Now, for her private patch, a pretty border of flowers would be a nice start – she doesn't mind replanting throughout the year as she can learn from her mistakes. Her best bets are primulas and bulbs such as crocus and daffodils in the spring, followed by asters, African daisies and nigella in the summer, and then some flowering pansies in autumn. Typical beginner's vegetables are broad beans and carrots as well as herbs like rosemary, bay, sage, thyme and parsley. According to folklore, the latter only grows in a house where the woman wears the trousers; here, of course, it thrives.

The Bobo Mission Statement

I .... knowingly identify myself
as an **BoBo Housewife.** And I am **DESPERATE.**

• • • • • • • • • • •

I hereby acknowledge my faults: that I am jealous of my
husband and his flourishing career, that I'm finding it
hard to control my unruly brood but am ashamed to
admit it, and that although I'd love to hire a nanny, my
jealousy couldn't cope with it. Too young, too pretty
– too much spousal temptation.

• • • • • • • • • • •

I do solemnly declare that in order to be less desperate,
I will be more open with my husband – after all, we pride
ourselves on being the best of friends – and admit that
although I may have managed my office with panache,
managing a household is an entirely different matter.

• • • • • • • • • • •

• • • • • • • • • • • •

In five years time I will have started working again part-time – not every woman's cut out to be a full-time mum. I will also start spending more time on my appearance, reminding Mr BoBo precisely why he married me in the first place. I may even learn how to properly apply kohl.

• • • • • • • • • • • •

And if I achieve my goals, I will treat myself (and my husband) to … a fortnight in a suite at the Ebony Lodge (a four-poster bed and plunge pool in the shade of jackalberry trees – what bliss!) at the Singita Private Game Reserve in South Africa. Since any period longer than an hour in a spa drives me mad, I can get my massages here – in the glorious outdoors – in between educational safari trips with the most knowledgeable of trackers and rangers. I won't even mind the 5am starts. Best of all? Kids under 12 aren't allowed in case they frighten the animals. Rejoice!

• • • • • • • • • • • •

The Hippie Housewife

3

She's flaky, artsy and oh-so adorable. Hence the endless stream of male admirers beating a path to her door — not that she notices — attracted by her free-spirited nature rather than her (lack of) homemaking skills. Good job she has such a capable daughter, then, isn't it?

The Hippie: A Chic Cinderella Story

In her twenties the Hippie was a babe: young, free and fun, the ultimate good-time girl. A decade later, she's a divorced single parent. Where did it all go wrong?

Actually, it hasn't gone nearly as wrong as she thinks. For a start, her taste – the epitome of boho chic – means she's the envy of suburbia. The Hippie's home is artfully ramshackle (although more ramshackle than she imagines), stuffed full of reclaimed antique furniture and vintage fabrics. As her name suggests, she's also impressively green – albeit as-long-as-it-doesn't-mess-too-much-with-my-aesthetic green. She eats organically and does ashtanga yoga. Heck, she's even thinking of buying a Toyota Prius (Cameron Diaz's car, and she loves Cam – her style, her laissez-faire attitude, everything) but makes do with a suitably quirky Citroen 2CV. She also loathes housework – you'd never have guessed! – and claims her idol is Simone de Beauvoir, who once declared: 'Few tasks are more like the torture of Sisyphus than housework, with its endless repetition.'

Really, though, her idol is Cinderella (minus the down-on-her-knees scrubbing). Really, she wants to be saved by a seriously-rich-yet-still-kind-to-animals second husband. Underneath the carefree façade is an aspiration to yummy-mummy-dom: she dreams of the big house and the sprawling family. She may have no end of admirers but the pool is somewhat limited: the opportunistic postman, the too-good-to-be-true plumber or the occasional dinner date with a desperate divorcee, thanks to her well-meaning matchmaker friends. Hardly husband material, alas. The search goes on …

Her cocktail

La Vie en Rose: pink champagne, rose water, crushed strawberries and a sugar cube. It's pretty and pink and, despite everything, the Hippie truly believes life is rosy.

Her knickers

Chaste-yet-seductive cream lace shorties with lilac bows from London label Myla – she remembers reading one that Kate Moss is a fan.

Her shoes

A pair of Swedish ShoFolk boots – known in the trade as 'the new Uggs' (she was too PC for Mukluks, the original 'new Uggs' which were made from bunny fur).

Her handbag

A 'porthole' bag in a bold floral print from New York label Neal Decker. A modern twist on the carpetbag: big enough to sling everything in; handmade for that crucial homespun feel.

The Hippie Kitchen

The Hippie hates housework. She's what Florence Nightingale, a huge fan of hygiene, would have called a 'flapper' – an ineffectual and inconsistent cleaner. She believes that after the first four years, dust doesn't get any worse, and never, ever cleans the oven – the dirt will eventually burn off, won't it? Indeed, dust bunnies have been lurking behind her fridge for so long they're practically pets.

And cooking? Forget it – the microwave is her (and her teenage daughter's) best friend. Despite this, her kitchen is super-stylish. Her passion for keeping up with yummy-mummy fashions mean she has all the domestic paraphernalia *du jour*: an artful array of freestanding kitchen furniture that includes a reclaimed Butler's sink (on which she keeps smashing glasses), shabby chic Cabbages & Roses curtains, deliberately mismatched crockery and, thanks to her tree-hugger side, Ecover cleaning products from Fresh & Wild. Unopened. Her one concession to gadgetry is a juicer. Not any old juicer, mind, but a dual-speed-motor Breville JE3 Professional Juice Extractor. That's what all the glossies recommend, after all.

How not to be Desperate Tip

The key to domestic bliss is little and often. Psychological research proves that a clean house helps clear the mind. So, if the Hippie starts adhering to this philosophy, then her life will become a whole lot easier.

The Hippie Bedroom

Hurrah! The bedroom is where the Hippie's artistic tendencies can run unbridled. Without the watchful eye of her daughter reigning in her taste, she can go craft-crazy. Hence the distressed furniture, bric-a-brac finds – and are those her *own* doodles decorating the walls? Of course!

Bedchamber chic

At the moment (perhaps unsurprisingly, she changes this room more often than her filter coffee paper), there's a Hampton's vibe. She's cleverly constructed a bed from some storm-damaged tree trunks and strewn a stripy blanket from cashmere label Brora casually over the end. Her bedclothes are antique embroidered linen plucked from European flea markets – Parisian ones are her favourites. This is a wise investment: she knows good linen lasts a lifetime, certainly longer than her bedroom themes. Caring for linen is the only thing her mother taught her that she actually took on board. She washes it in cool water using soap flakes, rinses well, stores in tissue paper, and then damp irons before use.

After-hours attire

As her love of cashmere shows, the Hippie is a nester, but there are no unsexy winceyette pyjamas for her, oh no! Her cocooning must be done in style and in labels devoted to loungewear, ideally a Moroccan-style pure linen djellaba dressing gown from Toast and stripy pink pjs in soft-washed cotton from Hush.

What's on her nightstand?

Even though there's a bookshelf behind her bed – she copied the look from Carrie Bradshaw's bedroom and often has anxiety dreams about it collapsing in the night – most of her literary finds are stacked by the bed.

She's not averse to the odd self-help book, especially ones relating to men. Her current fave is *He's Just Not That Into You: The No-Excuses Truth to Understanding Guys* by Greg Behrendt and Liz Tuccillo, a book that explains loud and clearly why he hasn't called; this stops her obsessing so much. Other must-haves include *Live Alone and Like It* by Marjorie Hillis, reissued from 1936 and including such gems as 'The pleasures of a single bed', and *The Good Shopping Guide* to aid her attempts to become a more conscientious consumer. Oh, and a somewhat dog-eared copy of *Pride and Prejudice* – of course.

How not to be Desperate Tip

A string of fairy lights is the Hippie's idea of secondary lighting. This is not enough! Proper secondary lighting is crucial for boudoir calm. Her best bet is an overhead dimmer, which might sound naff and a throwback to the Eighties, but 100-watt strip lighting is hardly seductive. The ideal bedside light, on the other hand, should be conical in shape and with a head that aims at her book – and nothing else.

The Hippie Wardrobe

The Hippie is a masterclass in looking deliberately deshabillé. She looks totally un-put-together, without a sartorial care in the world, but in reality has spent hours of anguish in front of the mirror. Her wardrobe staples are ethnic in inspiration and hint at exotic travel. She's also a fan of mixing old with new, especially if it's her teenage daughter's high-street finds. The Hippie, then, is truly the fashion plate of suburbia.

Her can't-live-without labels

- Apsara. The Hippie loves a bejewelled, fitted kaftan; Apsara does them better than anyone else.

- Matthew Williamson, whose barely-there chiffon camisoles are to-die-for and ideal for her usual uniform of jeans-and-a-nice-top.

- Day Birger et Mikkelsen. The girl can't get enough of the Danish label's pretty printed skirts and disc-detail jewellery.

- Antik Batik, especially their sequinned-toed moccasins and cotton kurtas. *So* Marrakesh, by-way-of-Goa.

An instant cure for iron-o-phobics

Other than her beloved antique linen, the Hippie never irons. 'Soooo tedious!' she moans. But ironing needn't be such a chore. To get the best results, clothing should first be spritzed with a water spray – slightly damp garments provide the most satisfying results. Delicate fabrics should be ironed over a layer of tissue paper to avoid damage. A sneaky cheat is to use a steam bath – garments hung in a hot bathroom, especially ones made from velvet, will quickly de-crease. However, the Hippie should never get overzealous and start ironing her underwear – life really is too short.

The Hippie Bathroom

The Hippie's beauty motivation? To look the glowing picture of natural good health – without any assistance whatsoever. She'd like to think she can leave the house in nothing more than a slather of Burt's Beeswax lipbalm; in reality, though, looking good requires plenty of clever products – and cruelty-free ones at that. She once read that 60 per cent of anything applied to the skin is absorbed into the body … and freaked out. By rights she should be crouching over an African river, Anita Roddick-style, using the extract of some indigenous plant for her cleanser. Since this is not always possible, instead she stuffs her bathroom cabinet full of organic products. Just the way nature intended.

The essentials

Lipstick: Gypsy Soirée, a pretty pink colour from Fresh. **Moisturizer:** REN Rose Complex, which is 100 per cent natural, plus she gets a healthy flush from Nuxe's Huile Prodigieuse rubbed into her cheeks. **Scent:** Kiehl's Grapefruit, an alcohol-free fragrance that's as fresh as it gets. **Her secret beauty tip:** Dr Hauschka's cleansing cream. The Hippie likes to think she's sensitive both outside and in, and this is one of the gentlest cleansers on the market.

You are what you juice

The Hippie solves any complexion worries with her juicer. Particular favourites are strawberries, blueberries, avocado and leafy green vegetables such as spinach. Back in her bathroom cabinet are a variety of vitamin supplements such as vitamin E, crucial for healthy skin, and starflower oil rich in gamma linolenic acid (GLA) to perk up a peaky complexion.

How not to be Desperate Tip

To be perfectly ethical, the Hippie should think about packaging (boxes, cellophane, fancy bottles) before she buys. Better still, phone up beauty companies and ask about refills. She'd be shocked at how many actually offer them, especially perfume manufacturers – most of the cost of a bottle of scent goes on the actual bottle itself.

A Wrinkle-reducing eye mask

The Hippie would never consider cooking anything in the kitchen, but might be tempted with a little mixing in the bathroom. Here she uses yoghurt (which contains the same active ingredients as commercial AHAs) and even beats egg whites (excellent for oily skin). The following recipe is her favourite all-natural solution for softening lines around the eyes.

Mix all the ingredients together and gently pat on to the skin around the eyes. Leave for 15 minutes. Rinse with warm water.

1 tsp aloe vera gel
1 tsp ground almonds
1 tsp chamomile tea
(made from a
herbal infusion)

The Hippie's Exercise Routine

In the gym the Hippie thinks Christy Turlington. Yoga is her exercise of choice, but only if she has the right gear. She therefore insists on head-to-toe Nuala, Christy's clothing range, accessorized with a mat from trendy new-age label Calmia. She burns nag champra incense sticks (like the pros), and once threatened to turn the spare bedroom into a bikram-style 105-degree hot room (until her daughter talked her out of it).

The matching mat-and-bag combo is a dead giveaway though: the Hippie is hardly a yoga purist. As much as she claims she intends to wake at 5am every morning to start practising her moves, in reality she a fair-weather yoga-ite and will never, ever master the headstand. The following moves, however, will help her feel more like she's been bombed by the om.

The triangle

This stretches the spine. Stand with your feet four steps apart and turn your right foot 90 degrees to the right. Inhale and raise both arms until they are shoulder level and parallel to the floor. Exhale and turn your head to the right. Inhale and stretch your right arm down your right leg as far as it will go. Rest your right hand on your calf while your left arm points straight up. Take several deep breaths. Inhale and straighten up. Exhale and lower your arms. Repeat on the other side.

The downward dog

Get down on your hands and knees, hands shoulder-distance apart, knees hip-distance apart. Inhale and curl your toes under. Exhale and lift your knees off the floor and straighten your legs. Push upwards with your arms, keeping your spine straight. You should be strengthening your spine while keeping your legs straight and your feet flat on the ground. Keep your arms and shoulders in alignment with your spine and hold your head between your arms. Maintain the position for a few breaths, then place your knees on to the floor and sit back on your heels.

The Hippie's Love and Sex Life

Due to her single status, the Hippie still dates, which means she somehow has to convince a gentleman to ask her out in the first place. Her neighbourhood nemesis is the local never-been-married man-eater who has flirting down to an art; the Hippie, on the other hand, is somewhat out of practice. Not to worry: flirts are bred, not born.

How to be an incurable flirt

- Make an entrance. A good flirt should have presence, so the Hippie must pause for a beat when she enters a room, put her shoulders back, then continue.

- Maximize eye contact. The Hippie should look at the object of her affection for a little longer than is usual, and then seductively lower her eyes.

- Mirror body language. She sould paying special attention to where her feet are pointing.

- Reveal the inner wrist, a gesture that is said to make a woman appear instantly vulnerable – and ripe for seduction.

- Aim for an 'accidental' touch – the Hippie and her intended both reach for a door handle at the same time. Sparks are will fly.

And Sex?

Oh, my! The Hippie is a tad out of practice here, so when a gentleman caller lingers later than was originally intended, she could find herself feeling excited … and also scared. In case she's forgotten what to do – which she's convinced herself is the case – here are a few pointers …

Tentative foreplay

The setting should be conducive, the clichés rolled out: soft lighting, scented candles, and no disturbances. Sexpert Lou Paget states that 'kissing is the number one thing that gets women's motors running'. Men, of course, see it merely as a finger-tapping prelude to the main course – but that doesn't mean the Hippie can cut corners. Her kissing should start slow and stay that way: she needs to relax, pace herself and stay in sync with her gentleman caller's actions.

How not to be Desperate Tip

If this doesn't feel too forward, the Hippie could put a chunk of ice in her mouth without her gentleman caller knowing. Then kiss him all over, gradually allowing the ice to touch his skin. How daring!

Out-of-practice sex

Enthusiasm goes a long way – as does a generous glug of wine. The key is keeping it simple, so the Hippie should forget whipping out the *Karma Sutra* and stick to the missionary position. Communication is also important – he will probably be as nervous as she is. The Hippie might consider that men are particularly stimulated by visuals (women respond better to what they hear or feel), so if she keeps the lights on, she could very well drive him wild – and drive herself to the nearest pillow for a strategic cover-up. And, if it's *still* a bit of a disaster, she should laugh it off and remember: practice makes perfect, telling him just that.

First Date Dos

	Dream date	Pre-date preparation	What to wear
Lunch date	Matthew Kassovitz in *Amélie*.	Lots of clever makeup and a hat – when it comes to first impressions, natural daylight can be unforgiving.	A style that says, 'I may look like I haven't made an effort – but I have!' Think jeans, a shrunken jacket, and smart-but-sexy top.
Picnic date	Jude Law in The Talented Mr Ripley.	Minimal makeup such as i.d. bareMinerals foundation that contains sunscreen plus oil of citronella to keep bugs at bay.	Think layers: maybe a chunky cardie concealing a sexy top, teamed with Capri pants, plimsolls and a floppy hat.
Drinks date	Humphrey Bogart in Casablanca.	A piping hot bath to boost her complexion and a champagne cocktail to boost her confidence.	Something pretty and chiffon-y by Chloé and strappy silver heels.
Dinner date	George Peppard in *Breakfast at Tiffany's*.	A snack: chances are you'll be too nervous to eat.	A suitably subtle little black dress (Chanel still do the best) balanced with go-for-broke jewellery.

... and Don'ts

Where to go	Do	Don't
Somewhere with an after-hours feel, even at midday, such as a brasserie like the Wolseley in London or Balthazar's in Manhattan.	Gen up on the latest films/exhibitions/gossip. Spontaneous small talk can be tricky.	Make a bee-line for the drinks menu. You may be gagging for a tipple but binge drinking isn't chic before 6pm.
A pretty patch of green – as long as it offers the necessary foliage cover. Things might get steamy …	Look interested when he turns into Nature Boy and starts speaking at length on the different types of oak.	Wear spike heels, unless the lawn needs aerating.
A sleek hotel bar – low-level lighting, guaranteed seating, and all those bedrooms a mere elevator-ride away.	Be adventurous and sample exotic cocktails from the menu. The hotel's mixologist is bound to be first-class.	Start suggestively jangling room keys. Far too obvious – he might run a mile.
The perfect date food is anything a couple can share. Think Asian street food or fancy tapas.	Gaze adoringly when he attempts to order a bottle of Chateau Latour in terrible Français.	Order the salad, even if that's all you want.

The Hippie's Home Life

The Hippie is a self-confessed self-help junkie – yet somehow, even after assimilating all that pop-psychology, she's no closer to taking the road less travelled. Lucky for her, then, that unlike most of the ladies on her lane, her home life is relatively angst-free. As a desperate housewife, though, it's nowhere near perfect. She still has her 'issues', as she calls them, but they're all entirely solvable.

Issue One: Acting more like a mother than a friend

This is the Hippie's biggest problem: she's desperate to be her daughter's best friend, partly because she's trying to be as little like her own mother – an old-school disciplinarian – as possible, and partly because she still feels she's 17.

Well, she isn't. Indeed, the Hippie is not an isolated case: commonly known as 'Saffy Syndrome', after the mature daughter versus kidult mother in the TV series *Absolutely Fabulous*, there's a whole generation of artsy mothers who openly talk to their offspring about sex and soft-drugs while borrowing freely from their Britney-inspired wardrobes.

The Hippie should remember that her daughter doesn't need another friend, especially one who wears age-inappropriate low-rise jeans. She needs a mother. The Hippie could start taking some of those self-help phrases on board, then, 'adopting appropriate boundaries' and the like. She should also stop encouraging her daughter to date every boy on the block. Maybe she's just not ready.

Issue Two: Introducing her new boyfriend to her daughter

The Hippie's daughter is not a child; she's not going to buy the 'mummy's special friend' line. The Hippie should therefore be wholly honest about her relationship with this new man, but she should wait until she has some level of commitment: teenagers crave stability, so it's no good if he's there one day, gone the next.

If her daughter reacts badly, it's only because she's never had to share her mother before. The Hippie must therefore be patient and keep activities with this new man separate from those with her daughter. Eventually, though, it's more than likely the daughter will feel as if a weight has been lifted from her shoulders. Why? Because the wayward Hippie's support network is no longer restricted to just her.

As for this new man, under no circumstances should the loved-up housewife start asking him to take on paternal duties. It's not his job – and, besides, he'll probably vanish in a flash.

Issue Three: Dealing with her ex-husband's new girlfriend

She should, of course, do this with a benevolent smile on her face. Yet, inside, she'll be a seething mass of bitterness and jealousy. How dare he get over her? How dare he move on?

Any false hopes she ever had of the two of them getting back together have been cruelly quashed. However, after the initial shock – and some serious mulling – she should feel liberated. Only now can she achieve closure, any self-help junkie's idea of utopia.

Issue Four: Being utterly and – let's face it – inexcusably disorganized all of the time

Scattiness is adorable … up to a point. Then it becomes irritating, for the Hippie herself as well as for everyone else around her. However, spring-cleaning one's life can easily be equated with spring-cleaning one's soul, a concept the Hippie adores. If her house is less cluttered, she'll instantly feel more like the mistress of her destiny – after all, if she can't reign in the dust under her sofa, how on earth can she hope to control her own fate?

Life coaches believe there are three ways even the most messy of people can instantly become more organized:

1. Start writing lists. Prioritize your 'To Do' list, the main areas of your life in need of improvement, and include possible solutions.

2. But don't be a slave to your list! You can never hope to achieve everything on your list, so make it as realistic as possible.

3. Stop wasting time trying to control the uncontrollable – moaning about the rain, for instance – and instead focus your energies on mending your washing machine. At last.

Hippie Entertaining

As a single gal, the Hippie's girlfriends mean the world to her. It's the one time she project manages a night in together. But what to do? And, more importantly, what to serve? This is when her culinary un-expertise reveals itself to the world – or at least to her neighbours. Alas, her usual mac-and-cheese won't cut it; *gourmet* comfort food, on the other hand, will make her front-page news in the next neighbourhood newsletter.

What to do

The Hippie believes entertaining should be fun, so no smug couples, no place cards and no girl-boy-girl seating mentality. She won't fret too much about her dirty house – she figures that the right lighting (ie, hundreds of scattered tea-lights) and enough alcohol should conceal the mess. First things first, though: the music, ideally something chilled in keeping with her character. She needs to up the ante on the usual Air/Zero 7 dinner-party background muzak – *Colour The Small One* by Sia (a former vocalist with Zero 7, in fact) is much more unexpected.

Now, the drinks. The Hippie is keen for her guests to remain well-lubricated, but to prove she's made the effort, she should choose her wine carefully. Chardonnay is too old hat; pinot noir too everyday. She needs something more exotic, then, like rosé. Highly recommended is Charles Melton's Rosé of Virginia, which is scrumptiously fruity and a gorgeous deep pink colour to boot.

Hippie Menu

Easy roast chicken

Set the oven at 230°C/450°F/Gas 8. Place the chicken in a roasting tin and cover with butter and lemon juice. Season with herbes de Provence, salt and pepper. Add the garlic cloves and stuff the lemon shells inside the rib cage. Roast for 15 minutes, then turn the

2kg/4½lb organic chicken
75g/2½ oz unsalted butter
Juice of 1 lemon
Handful of herbes de Provence
Salt and freshly ground pepper
3 garlic cloves, unpeeled

oven down to 190°C/375°F/Gas 5. Baste the bird, then roast for another 45 minutes, basting twice more during roasting. The bird is cooked when the juices run clear (with a skewer). Place the cooked chicken on a warm serving plate and leave to rest for 10 minutes. Serve with a green salad.

Crunchy chocolate mousse

Break the chocolate into pieces and melt with the brandy, coffee and cocoa powder. While the mixture is still warm, whisk in the egg yolks one at a time. Whisk the egg whites into stiff peaks and fold into the chocolate mixture. Whip the cream into peaks and fold into the mixture. Setting aside

75g/2½ oz plain chocolate (at least 70 per cent cocoa solids)
1 tbsp brandy
1 tbsp cold strong black coffee
½ tbsp cocoa powder
2 eggs, separated
75ml/3fl oz double cream
25g/1oz crushed amaretti biscuits

some crushed biscuits for decoration, place the remainder at the bottom of four ramekins. Cover with mousse and chill in the fridge for 3 hours. Before serving, sprinkle with the leftover biscuits.

Hippie Escapes

The Hippie sees herself as an alternative jetsetter and simply adores travelling to far-flung lands – even though her motive may be to expand her home décor as much as her mind. Of course, the hippie trail has changed greatly since the Sixties; today's nouveau hippies wear Etro kaftans, stay in boutique hotels and do yoga at sunrise in the company of fashion designers and the odd enlightened celeb. The Hippie knows this – and laps it up. After all, she wouldn't be seen dead in a saffron-hued ashram robe and can't stand mung beans. And for once her daughter doesn't mind – at least it means she returns with some nice presents …

1. Goa, India

The vibe: A blend of bliss mixed with smug self-satisfaction – you can live like a king on next to nothing.

Who goes? A mix of savvy media types and rose-tinted aging hippies.

What to do: Chill out, dolphin watch, star spot (Kate Moss and her posse hang out here).

What to say: 'I'm just off to get my hands henna-ed.' However naff it may be at home, here henna is de rigueur.

Where to stay: Bhakti Kutir at the southern-most tip of Goa's most unspoilt beach, Palolem, a collection of eco-friendly thatched bamboo huts. Guests are offered yoga and meditation classes daily; there is also an Ayurvedic masseur and superb organic food.

2. Byron Bay, Australia

The vibe: Laid-back yet boho chic. Birkenstocks are fine … as long as they're a limited-edition pair of white Gizehs.

Who goes? Antipodean celebs like Nicole Kidman, Russell Crowe and Naomi Watts, whose mother owns a house here.

What to do: Surf, shop at the hippie market, or visit the Ambaji Wellness Centre for a cranio sacral balancing treatment.

What to say: 'I love *all* animals, even snakes.' Wildlife fanatics are big here, too, so don't go killing any spiders.

Where to stay: Byron Blisshouse is the luxe option: set in tropical gardens, it has a wide range of sumptuous treatments to choose from – think deep-tissue massages, Dr Hauschka facials and full-body wraps. Ahhhh …

The Hippie Garden

The Hippie firmly believes her garden should be her sanctuary, and rightly so: why must she toil when a garden exists to be enjoyed? Despite her hippie charms and aspirations to earth mother-dom, she's as un-green-fingered as they come.

Her horticultural aim

She wants a gloriously informal garden overgrown in all the right places, but it must be easy to care for and stuffed full of plants that won't die. Her garden furniture complements this: shabby chic reclaimed French café chairs and ornate-yet-elegantly-rusting metal tables.

Perfect plants

The Hippie needs plenty of hardy perennials – for instance, candytuft, Chinese lantern, day lilies and thrift (sea pink). These will thrive whatever the season, so she won't have to bother replanting. A few evergreens wouldn't go amiss either, maybe azaleas or heather. For more colour, she should plant pretty flowering shrubs and bushes – lilac, Japanese mahonia and laburnum are perfect – remembering to add perennial ground cover (little plants that spread, like creeping jenny) between each shrub.

How not to be Desperate Tip

A cute herb garden in her window box would be handy for all those fresh herbs she constantly forgets to buy. Least likely to die are rosemary and thyme.

The Hippie Mission Statement

I .... knowingly identify myself
as an **Hippie Housewife**. And I am **DESPERATE**.

• • • • • • • • • • •

I hereby acknowledge my faults: that I am self-obsessed,
flaky, sluttish (in a hygienic sense), lacking in self-esteem,
too concerned with self-validation via celebrities, and
don't do nearly as much yoga as I claim.

• • • • • • • • • • •

I do solemnly declare that in order to be less desperate,
I will be less consumed with yummy-mummy envy, less
reliant on my daughter – start acting more like a mother,
less like a friend – cut down on my self-help habit and learn
to be more poised on first dates – after all, I know I'm still
a babe, especially when the man sitting opposite me in a
restaurant is losing his hair and developing a paunch.

• • • • • • • • • • •

• • • • • • • • • • • •

In five years time I will have sorted out my 'hobby job', making it less of a hobby, more of a job. I'll go on a business course, move my operation from the kitchen table to the spare room – oooh, a proper office at last! – and devise a strategy plan, which I swear I'll stick to. Oh, and if by then I still haven't found my prince, I won't worry. Honest.

• • • • • • • • • • • •

And if I achieve my goals, I will treat myself (and my daughter) to ... a fortnight at the Ananda Spa in the Himalayas, for pure pampering interspersed with a hefty dose of spirituality. Ayurveda, yoga, gourmet food, spectacular views, gentle trekking ... and I'm especially keen on the fact that the nearest town is Rishikesh, the town on the Ganges where the Beatles learnt to meditate in the Sixties; now, of course, packed with Western yoga bunnies armed with blue mats. Hippie heaven on a stick.

• • • • • • • • • • • •

The Trophy Housewife

She's a former model (albeit of the C-list variety) who's married well – and rich – Her spouse doesn't know she never wants children since it would ruin her figure. The barely legal gardener, on the other hand, is a *very* different matter …

The Trophy: A legend in her own mind

When faced with a dilemma – 'How can I explain my sky-high credit-card bill to my husband?' for instance – the Trophy copes by thinking: 'What would J-Lo do?' Like J-Lo, the Trophy is imbued with a sense of entitlement and would be delighted if her staff started addressing her as 'Milady' (her husband vetoed the idea). Her housewife heroines are Kimora Lee Simmons, the living embodiment of conspicuous consumption, and Joan and Jackie Collins, the living embodiments of ladies-who-lunch. Occasionally when her bad taste mechanism goes into overdrive, the Trophy wife is much more like Jackie Stallone, though. Her house is the epitome of nouveau naffness: lots of marble, gold taps galore and a pair of stone lions at the gates. She drives a Mercedes SLK 200 convertible and has a fluffy pomeranian whose sole exercise is accompanying her to the shops.

The Trophy is a legend in her own mind. She truly believes her life ought to be regularly documented by the paparazzi – she's by far the most glamorous (and secretly scandalous) person she knows – or should at the very least be a plotline for a daytime soap. Her neighbourhood nemesis? Unquestionably the local busy body who suspects she's been having multiple affairs (she has). The only time she does any housework, in fact, is to cover her tracks, and she can frequently be found mowing her lawn at midnight in nothing more than her knickers – proof that tabloid tactics *don't* always result in genuine glamour.

Her cocktail

A Horny Toad margarita.
When ordering from a
hunky bartender, she likes
to make the most of a
suggestive cocktail name.

Her knickers

Cosabella nude low-rise thong.
A die-hard G-string girl, she
knows this brand is the best.

Her shoes

Gina 4-inch Swarovski-
encrusted strappy sandals
with toenails painted
'Friar, Friar Pants on
Fire', a scandalously
scarlet shade by O.P.I.

Her handbag

A teeny, tiny satin Dior
'Flowers' bag with embroidered
detail plus – crucially –
unmissable 'C' and 'D'
dangling logos.

The Trophy Kitchen

The Trophy never sets foot in the kitchen except to lounge provocatively while the gardener trims her hedges outside. Or maybe to play some *9½ Weeks*-style sex games with her husband in a bid to increase the limit on her platinum credit card. Nevertheless, everything here is super-luxe like expensive pink Farrow & Ball walls and Italian black marble surfaces.

How to deal with staff

Knowing the correct etiquette in dealing with the hired help is a breeze if you're to the manor born. The Trophy, however, has clawed her way over from the wrong side of the tracks, so some advice might help smooth over the edges.

- Don't act like they're invisible and ignore them until something's gone missing – and then be all over them like a rash.

- Don't insist on them wearing a uniform if they don't want to – it's not *Gosford Park*.

- Do remember to pay staff, even when they're on holiday.

- Do consider gifts at Christmas. Although the Queen famously gives her staff a pudding, the Trophy's housekeeper would probably be happier with cash.

How not to be Desperate Tip

To clean gold swan taps, wipe with a just-damp cloth. Never rub, and never, ever use metal polish or those swans might lose their lustre. (This tip should, of course, be dispensed to the cleaner.)

The Trophy Bedroom

If it were the Eighties, this room would be a monument to tacky excess: gaudy chandeliers, a mirrored ceiling, perhaps a vibrating waterbed. Thank goodness, then, that it's the 21st century and even the Trophy has had the foresight to chuck out the chintzy bedspread. Instead, the walls are painted a restful shade of lilac, while the only mirrors are Venetian and surprisingly tasteful. The artwork is a little more risqué: black-and-white photographs of couples having … um … is that legal? In any case, it's Art.

Befitting the queen she thinks she is, the bed is a four-poster, albeit a modern take on the traditional design: a white iron affair from Italian designers Cantori should do the job nicely. Her crib is covered in bespoke silk charmeuse sheets coupled with a profusion of pillows and cushions – enough, in fact, to lose someone. Or smother them.

Off-duty attire

A cami and shorts from Miami-based company Eberjey, a sexier, more up-to-date version of the negligée, which is too naff even for her; a generous layer of heavy-duty night cream; a satin marabou-trimmed eye mask; earplugs.

On-duty attire

For when she wants something – and will do just about anything to get it. A pair of Damaris silk corset pants: impractical for underwear but perfect for seduction, with a giant bow at the back ripe for unwrapping. The Trophy will also wake up early to brush her teeth and reapply her makeup. Frankly, Mr Trophy won't know what's hit him.

What's on her nightstand?

She's not much of a reader – in fact, she's never managed to finish a whole novel. The only book she owns, hidden away in a secret drawer, is *Seduction* by Robert Green, a tome that divulges machiavellian tactics for seducing anyone – and everyone. It's her manual for living. As is the great pile of fashion magazines in which she circles new outfits she plans on buying.

How to deal with a snorer

Most men snore and the Trophy's husband is no exception. He's too proud to visit a sleep specialist, so some solutions are needed.

- Throw out the pillows and suggest he sleeps using just the one. Better still, sleep with no pillows at all.

- Make him sleep on his tummy – snoring is much less likely to occur in this position.

- Buy him a remedy from the chemist: Snore Calm's Chin-Up Strips, for instance, will stop his mouth from opening so much.

- Stop him from drinking before bed. Alcohol results in the airway – ie, the tube between the nose, mouth and lungs – becoming too relaxed. Smoking can also be a problem.

The Trophy Wardrobe

This dolly bird cites shopping as her favourite hobby. Her style is ritzy and Beverly Hills in the evening – heck, it's pretty ritzy even if she's just popping to the post box – while for low-key lounging it has to be a hot-pink tracksuit. The Trophy's sartorial mantra is simple: nothing can ever be too short, too tight or too useless – she'd accessorize every inch of her body if she could.

Her can't-live-without labels

- Juicy Couture. Bright, fun and LA-like. She not only loves their tracksuits but also their iconic terrycloth sundress – in orange, please – for enticing the pool boy.

- Versace/Julien Macdonald. When entertaining her husband's boss, she needs her outfits to be slit-to-the-hip and with plunging necklines.

- Roberto Cavali. The king of slutty chic; the sultan of excess. She adores him.

- C&C California. The company that perfected the figure-hugging T-shirt made from sexy sheer cotton that hangs in all the right places.

Top-heavy chic

Although her boobs are not her own, she still needs to think about proportions. Salma Hayek – whose boobs *are* her own – is usually spot-on, and the Trophy should take notes. Corsets are a good start and designers like Vivienne Westwood produce collections most flattering for her frame. Her tops should only be fitted: V-necks and wrap-around styles suit her best. Trousers and jeans should always be boot-cut for balance.

How not to be Desperate Tip

To clean valuable gems, place in a bowl of water and washing-up liquid for a few minutes, brush gently with a toothbrush, rinse and then dry using the lowest setting on a hairdryer. Do not wash porous stones (opals, turquoise) or pearls. The best way to clean them is to wear them.

The Trophy Bathroom

The Trophy is in her element here. The bathroom is her mothership – she used to be a model, after all (and of the decidedly low-rent variety who did their own makeup). Her aim: to look luxurious. Big ozone-busting hair, terracotta tan, look-at-me lips. Since she never does any housework, she has weekly manicures. In fact, her beautician, nail technician and waxer are all on speed-dial. She adores polishes with names that match her moods; it's as close to self-awareness as she gets. O.P.I. are especially good for this: 'To Eros Is Human', for instance, a deep pink colour, or maybe pillar-box red 'Redipus' to complement her teenage lover's Oedipal tendencies.

When it comes to a beauty routine, the Trophy is pretty lazy – it's her nature, after all. Still, she's vainer now than she was in her youth, ever since she started noticing that the odd wrinkle no longer disappears after a night of naughtiness. She's not happy.

The essentials

Lipstick: Lady Danger, a bright coral red from MAC. **Moisturizer:** Nicholas Perricone's cosmeceutical Day Face Treatment. Anti-wrinkle guru Dr Perricone is her new-found god. **Scent:** Coco Chanel. Her signature scent must be heavy and sensual. **Her secret beauty tip:** Secret Divin Skin Perfecting Serum by Guerlain. This will illuminate her skin if she hasn't been getting enough sleep due to, um, 'extra-curricular activities'.

A Last-minute blow-out

The Trophy is hair-centric; Elnett is her best friend. She knows if she wants to look younger, she should start with her locks, and that blow-dried hair looks best. She usually goes to a salon, but sometimes there isn't time.

1. Towel-dry just-washed hair.

2. Apply a straightening balm (nu:u Straight Blow-dry Balm comes highly recommended) evenly to hair, paying special attention to the ends.

3. Comb through hair with fingers while gently drying on a low setting.

4. Pull hair into three sections, two at the sides and one at the back. Clip two sides up.

5. Select a small portion of hair from the unclipped section. Using a thick, round brush and beginning at the roots, gently pull the brush through the hair to the ends while drying. First pull the brush through the underside, then do the top.

6. Repeat with other sections of hair.

7. Finish off with a spritz of Charles Worthington's Dream Hair Looks Amazing Invisible Control Blow-Dry Spray.

The best fake tans

As much as the Trophy loves her sunbed, she also worries about wrinkles.

- Fake Bake. Currently the coolest tan, favoured by supermodels and actresses alike. The result is relatively light in colour.

- Twinkle Tan from Fantasy Tap. A deep colour with added glitter. Perfect for parties – totally tacky-tastic.

- California Speed Tan. Best for an instant quick spray.

- St Tropez. The brand that started the whole fake-tan renaissance. Scary initial colour – extremely dark – but the end result lasts a long time. Victoria Beckham's a fan.

The Trophy Exercise Routine

Pilates: you barely move and achieve amazing results. No wonder, then, that it's the exercise of choice for most supermodels (who usually do nothing more strenuous than lift a Marlborough Light). For the Trophy, the gym also offers plenty of potential for affairs.

In the end, pilates still seems too much like hard work, though. Instead, the Trophy has taken up facial exercises, basically pilates for the visage, which help prevent fine lines, jowly chins, and turkey necks. Exercising facial muscles has long been popular in Japan – and think how ageless most Japanese women appear. In any case, she reasons, why bother with 'real' exercise? There's always liposuction for the next time she's been overindulging on violet creams.

Moves for a five-minute facelift

The snarl

1. Look into a mirror. Put your teeth together, relax your lips, straighten your back and put your shoulders back.

2. Now slowly form your mouth into a snarl. You should be able to feel the muscles on either side of your nose.

3. Hold for a count of five.

4. Slowly return your mouth to its original position. Relax and breathe. Do this movement five times.

The pat

1. Again looking in the mirror, take the middle and ring fingers of both hands and apply to the eye sockets.

2. Starting at the bridge of the nose, run your fingers out towards the eyebrows, applying a moderate amount of pressure as you go. Continue around the cheekbones and back towards the nose.

3. Repeat five times.

The Trophy's Love and Sex Life

You've got to hand it to her: the Trophy is a world-class secret-keeper. Just as well really with the number of flings she's had in her time, most recently with her jailbait gardener. She's fought every sinew in her body to spill the beans; even her girlfriends have no idea. Still, her confidence is making her slap-dash – she needs to be more careful if she doesn't want to get sprung.

How to have an affair (and not get caught)

- Choose carefully. Have a fling with someone who doesn't want to settle down. Commitment-phobes are perfect, as is someone already attached who has as much to lose as you.

- Meet your new lover out of town, somewhere there's guaranteed to be no one you know.

- Pay for everything in cash to avoid any suspect credit-card bills.

- Never, ever bring him home – or give him your home phone number.

- Store his number in your mobile under an alias, preferably using a woman's name. That way, if your partner sees a message coming in and a name flashes up, he won't get suspicious.

- Also, leave your cell phone on silent – your partner will never know about the unusually large volume of calls/messages you are suddenly receiving.

- Destroy all evidence. Never keep anything in writing: no letters, cards, texts, emails, nothing.

- Don't start trying out new moves in the bedroom – or have a sudden change of image.

- Always use a condom: the most obvious giveaway is an STD.

And how the Trophy can tell if her husband's been doing the dirty on her ...

Not that she wouldn't deserve it, but the last thing she wants is for her cash-cow husband to skip off into the sunset with a younger model. Well, *has* he been cheating? There are some classic telltale signs.

- He starts encouraging the Trophy to go to the gym – or worse, to see a therapist. He's trying to change her – or trying to prove to himself that he's *tried* to change her.

- Or *he* starts going to the gym, or buying swanky new clothes.

- He criticizes her more often than usual and for the niggliest of reasons.

- His friends start acting suspiciously round her – do they know something she doesn't?

- He suddenly becomes more secretive about his job, and starts working away more often.

Sex: How to perform the perfect fellatio

The Trophy's sexual prowess is legendary, her knowledge of moves encyclopedic. She knows there's one sure way to guarantee her man never strays, though: give great head. Of course, she's already a pro – she could give lessons – but every girl could do with a few pointers. In the interests of decency (something the Trophy knows nothing about), forthwith the Trophy will be referred to as a 'princess', the gentleman her 'knight' – and his you-know-what his 'sword' …

1. The princess should start slowly at the base of the sword and tease her way to the top, licking and fluttering her tongue as she goes.

2. She should pay special attention to the V-shaped split on the underside of his sword head, the most sensitive part of his sword. She may also consider using her hands to massage the, um, cannonballs near the sword.

3. The princess should then put the top of the sword in her mouth. She should cover her teeth with her lips and gently suck while making a ring around the sword's base with her thumb and forefinger.

4. She should then start gliding the sword in and out of her mouth. She could try licking with the back of her tongue too, not just the tip – it's a totally different sensation. More than anything, though, she shouldn't be repetitive and instead mix it up and move her mouth around.

5. Most of all, she should appear enthusiastic. If she doesn't feel like doing it, she shouldn't. He'll respect her for it – he's a knight, after all.

The Trophy's Home Life

The Trophy's home life is a battleground, and it's entirely her own doing. From day one, she's viewed her marriage as a game, a series of cunning strategies and tactical moves. Her husband is a man she must conquer – and one who gives as good as he gets. This can't continue. Sooner or later the Trophy will stop exploding – and start imploding. Which is *so* not a good look. The best way to deal with her home life, then, is to compare it to something with which she can relate, something close to her heart. Like handbags. Well, it *is* known as emotional baggage, after all.

The hard-as-nails Samsonite baggage: Constantly competing with her husband

The Trophy readily admits to enjoying a relationship that's a challenge and an uphill struggle; she thinks it's healthy to release her inner diva on an hourly basis. Why can't she stop? Mainly because she worries the excitement will vanish once the arguments cease – after all, making up is so much fun.

This is a difficult rut to get out of. She needs to start gradually. Instead of snide comments, she should try a few compliments – from the heart as opposed to those loaded with an ulterior motive. Life at home will become blissful. Then again, if they start getting along all the time, she could get away with even *more* murder.

The battered Mulberry baggage: Dealing with a toxic mother-in-law

Her in-laws are *so* not the parents she never had. She must therefore learn to bite her tongue – as long as she's married, she'll have a mother-in-law to contend with. One golden rule she should remember is to never, ever put her spouse in the middle of an in-law argument. Similarly, she shouldn't get her in-laws involved if there's any marital discord.

To smooth over relations, the Trophy should try to get to know her mother-in-law on a one-to-one basis – in other words, as someone other than the woman who married her precious little boy. If this doesn't help, the Trophy is allowed to play this toxic woman at her own game: turn the other cheek and start showering her with praise, something that will freak her out no end.

The Bill Amberg baby-care sheepskin baggage: Not wanting to start a family (while her husband does)

Hmmmm, shouldn't they have discussed this *before* walking down the aisle? If they did and he's still hoping she'll change her mind (she won't), marriage counselling might be a solution: this is an issue that greatly affects their future plans, together.

Remember, though, that the Trophy shouldn't feel ashamed that she doesn't want to be a mother – not everyone wants to; not everyone is cut out for motherhood, even. However, she should ask herself why she doesn't want kids – many people who dislike children often change their mind when the children are theirs. Maybe she could try to get some experience with kids – volunteer at a charity, perhaps (very un-her, but the out-of-character change could do her good), and suggest her husband does the same. Who knows: with any luck, it will actually put *him* off.

The vulgar Vuitton baggage: Reining in her conspicuous consumption

The Trophy is a shopaholic supreme. Since she doesn't have to worry about money – even her über-spending won't leave them on skid row – she thinks she doesn't have a problem. But why the constant craving? What's missing in her life?

Who knows, but there are a number of ways she can curb her spending. For a start, she can leave her credit cards at home – shopping with cash isn't nearly so easy or so satisfying. She could also try shopping with a friend – this might give her a soupçon of self-control, especially if her friend discourages her from unwise purchases – and before buying, she should pause and think, 'Do I really need this?' Honestly, it helps.

It might please the Trophy to know that psychologists believe a healthy marriage is one that involves a partner who's a spendthrift balancing out another partner who's thrifty. If both spend too much, it would be a financial disaster; if both are miserly, it will lead to a life of misery. Still, this isn't a licence for her to start spending even more.

Trophy Entertaining

When entertaining the boss, Mr Trophy knows better than to suggest a sit-down dinner. His wife will refuse point-blank. Instead, he thought he'd compromise with a drinks party – but the Trophy's still not happy. She's not even sure what these 'amuse-bouches' he keeps mentioning actually are.

What to do

A successful drinks party is not as easy as it appears. For a start, the Trophy must make sure she owns enough seats – not everyone will want to stand around talking. She should also consider adding some private areas for discreet tête-à-têtes. She then needs to think carefully about food: the perfect canapé is one that's small enough to disappear in a couple of bites plus comfortable to consume holding a glass *and*, quite possibly, a clutch bag, so no messy mini-burgers.

The Trophy would do well to greet her guests with a glass of champagne. Bling is best, in particular hip-hop favourite (and her own) Cristal. If she's slumming it with a supermarket brand – and there's

How not to be Desperate Tip

Since she's so me-me-me, it's tempting for the Trophy to forget when *she's* the one who's been entertained to send a thank-you note. The correct form is to write in proper ink – not biro – on a stiff card. Personalized correspondence cards should do very nicely. And will impress the neighbours no end.

nothing wrong with that – she can jazz it up with a Funkin fruit purée. These marvellous pure-fruit purées come in a variety of flavours – raspberry, white peach and passion fruit, for instance – and have long been an insider tip with mixologists. She will also need red and white wine, still and sparkling water, and a decent non-alcoholic alternative – a mocktail, perhaps? She should estimate around half a bottle of wine per person for a two-hour party. As for canapés, aim for six to eight per person.

Trophy Menu

A dead-simple canapé: Edamame with sea salt

These Japanese green bean nibbles are readily available in Oriental supermarkets (both fresh and frozen) and taste great hot with Maldon sea salt. Add edamame beans to a pan of slightly salted boiling water and return to the boil. Cook until the beans are tender – around 3 minutes. Drain and serve with flakes of sea salt.

An Intermediate level canapé: Camembert baked in its box

This is the sort of dish the Trophy's mother would have served in the 1970s – but that doesn't make it any less appealing. Place the cheese – minus any wrappings and any paper that might be attached to the wooden box – inside the box in an oven preheated to 190°C/375°F/Gas 5. Bake until the cheese is soft in the middle; this should take around 20–30 minutes. Remove from the oven, whip off the lid and slice off the tough top rind with a knife. Serve with chunks of baguette, perfect for dipping.

Trophy Escapes

The Trophy craves the chance to take the weight off her sling-backs and perhaps indulge in a little hedonism in the evenings. Where better, then, than a trip to the world's most scene-y beaches?

1. Capri

Who goes? This tiny island off Italy's Neapolitan coast has been attracting the jet set since the 1950s. The current crop of Capri-ites includes Mario Testino and Nicole Kidman.

Perfect bikini: Italians do beach culture better than anyone else. A Pucci swimsuit shows that the Trophy has made an effort – and is hoping to make a statement.

Where to stay? The Grand Hotel Quisisana is chandelier-filled and suitably opulent.

What to do? Hang out – and pose – at the hippest beach club on the island, Fontelina in Faraglioni.

And in the evening? More Pucci prints, this time vintage, teamed with a pair of white jeans and high heels, perfect for the obligatory post-dinner promenade. By then the island will have lost all its tacky day-trippers – bliss!

2. St Tropez

Who goes? This once-sleepy fishing village on the French Riviera changed for good with the invasion of Bardot. Now the stars can't stay away: Naomi Campbell, Kylie and P Diddy are all regulars.

Perfect bikini: With buff bodies everywhere, even the Trophy needs all the help she can get. Malia Mills does the most miraculous bikinis for the most awkward (read: normal) of bodies. Accessorize with heels and jewellery – it's expected here, even on the beach.

Where to stay? Byblos, which has been *the* place to stay since the 1960s.

What to do? Lunch at Club 55, the in-spot and best place for a salad niçoise, before the Trophy blags her way on to the biggest boat.

And in the evening? Les Caves du Roy, a St Tropez institution, where she can boogie the night away with the Riviera roués.

3. Ibiza

Who goes? This Spanish Balearic island is popular with the beautiful people who like to party – Elle Macpherson, Jade Jagger, Kate Moss.

Perfect bikini: Bijou beachwear on the right side of hippie – white is the colour that best sums up the island – accessorized with an Emily Shoehorn sequinned bag.

Where to stay? A private villa, preferably on the neighbouring island of Formentera. Take a speedboat over to Ibiza.

What to do? Sunbathe … but not until after 3pm. Otherwise it will appear she hasn't been partying hard enough.

And in the evening? She should aim to wear white again. Café del Mar is the best place to watch the sunset and relax with a drink before a hard night's clubbing at Manumission is a must on Mondays. On Sundays, aim for Space.

The Trophy Garden

If she's honest, the only time the Trophy finds herself in the garden is when she's meeting the gardener for a secret assignation under the bird table. Nevertheless, like all the housewives on her street, she has a definite idea of what makes a garden perfect. Even if she doesn't appreciate her lawn and rose bushes, she still has her standards.

Her horticultural aim

On a purely selfish level, the Trophy wants her garden to be as sensual and sexy-smelling as possible. Style-wise, she prefers something formal with a discreet love seat – for obvious reasons.

Perfect plants

Gorgeous-smelling plants on the right side of luxury include sweet peas, which can be cut – by her maid – for flower displays, and perennial lilies. In fact, lilies are the one plant she absolutely insists on – but only because they look so suggestive. For sensory overload in the evenings, she needs nicotiana and patches of night-scented jasmine. Ideally, the love seat should be surrounded by elegant trelliswork entwined with purple-blue clematis.

How not to be Desperate Tip

The Trophy can indulge herself with an ornate water feature – fountain, lilies, carp, the lot. She's never going to have to worry about children falling in now, is she?

The Trophy Mission Statement

I _____ knowingly identify myself
as an **Trophy Housewife**. And I am **DESPERATE**.

• • • • • • • • • • • •

I hereby acknowledge my faults: that I am self-motivated,
self-obsessed, self-possessed, and can't keep my hands off
the gardener.

• • • • • • • • • • • •

I do solemnly declare that in order to be less desperate, I
will lay off the affairs, start appreciating my husband
more (really, he's not that bad), and cultivate more friends
– deep down I know it's not right that my closest pal is
Pippa, my Pomeranian.

• • • • • • • • • • • •

In five years time I will have embraced some serious soul-
searching and heavy-duty therapy (and not of the retail
variety). I might even have invested some of my energies
into helping those less fortunate than myself; maybe even

becoming a Queen of Hearts and volunteering for a charity. My new mantra? It's better to give than to receive.

● ● ● ● ● ● ● ● ● ● ● ●

And if I achieve my goals, I will treat myself to … a month ensconced in the Bath House at the Mandalay Bay Hotel in Las Vegas. A spa in Vegas? Totally Trophy – and this is one of the best in the world, with a dozen different types of massage, rose petal body wraps and volcanic treatments galore. The decor is tres rock star, with lots of muted earthy tones, and its sleek architecture has won awards. If I find temptation too hard to resist, the ritz and glitz of Vegas is just outside the doors. Although I'm not materialistic now, right?

● ● ● ● ● ● ● ● ● ● ● ●